THE LONELY BAR

Jared Reed

The Lonely Bar

First Edition: 2022

ISBN: 9781524316754
ISBN eBook: 9781524327897

© of the text:
    Jared Reed

© Layout, design and production of this edition: 2022
EBL

All rights reserved. No part of this publication may be reproduced, distributed, or transmitted in any form or by any means, including photocopying, recording, or other electronic or mechanical methods, without the prior written permission of the Publisher.

To anyone who reads these words and feels understood through this book, I will be comforted to know that I am not alone.

-Cheers to everyone

Table of contents

The Reminisce 11
The Hateful... 43
The Hope to Heal 77

Under the influence
People feel the love

Or hate

The hate always
Comes first naturally

Why can't love?

THE REMINISCE

Dancing Dreams

Thought after thought
Memory after memory
Viciously circling in mind
Revising events from the past
Or soon for the future

I feel these thoughts in my closed eyes
More than in my head
Will comfort me
While slowly drifting off in this bed

When the loneliness grows
People will fall for anyone
For anything
And claim it to be destined
All starting with a simple hello

But once the loneliness is gone
People will part ways
And act like their time spent
Was nothing more
Than time wasted

Heart struck

Your lavish silk purple bow
Caught my eye
It held your beautiful wavy brown hair
Who even knew?
A simple accessory would have my full attention
On you

Focusing from the top of your head
Then soon down to your face
I was struck instantly with fear
Attempting to compliment
Your stunning sparkling eyes
Quickly transitioned into frustration

Because of this woman
My drunken wandering thoughts
Forget to open the door for her
That I blocked
"Excuse yourself Mister" she spoke
Frantically I step aside
For the princess to open her own door

Today was the most
I've ever talked in awhile
Giving you a 'Good Evening"
While lighting a cigarette

Leading to her asking for one
Without hesitance we exchanged
I give her a drag
And she gives me a conversate

"You are a lifesaver. Stress is a killer lately"
"you've ever had days like that?"
Very clumsy
I was listening with my eyes
More than my ears
While her green eyes stood ground on me

Wondering in mind
This is a great start!
But how long
Will this relatable talk last?

-Conversation with a perfect stranger

I love these conversations
About what happened in each other's life
It helps to understand
How we ended up living this way

You said to me
Your parents made you this way
Another peer answers with
Losing a loved one scarred you

Understanding where anyone came from
I ordered shots on me
"Let's drink to forget!'
Mothers are not being mothers
Fathers are not being fathers
Life throws death every corner

We are what we are
Nothing will help to change
Or fix us
No human man or woman

-Can we still be saved?

This unforeseen night
Felt amazing
The minute She walked in
Her eyes would not leave my direction
Later
She approached me
Started complimenting my tight black shirt
Slowing leaning into
The scent of my cologne
While whispering into my ear
How she loved
My sharp face and powerful brown eyes

The next Friday night you arrived
Only this time
You seemed different
Your usual scent
Was covered by perfume
The lipstick you wore was a radiant bright red
Your outfit showed every single curve

I feared to compliment
Every lustful flaunt seen
But the most noticeable difference
About you tonight
Was the smile shown
And how big it was

As much as I want to speak to you again, I feel whatever we talk about will be about you; about YOUR day, problems, and plans.

Understanding I am a man to listen. I've spent months talking to you about nothing but you. Knowing everything from your favorite food, movies, and color.

The thought stings in my brain. That after this entire time, you've never once asked for my last name.

-easy for YOU, but never for ME

After what happened tonight
From this day on
I don't think I'll ever trust a soul

If ever you need my help
I will only help myself

You feel hungry
I will not feed you

If memories were ever kept
May they forever be erased

You ever call me
I will not pickup

Walking on the street one day
And you see me?
My back will be turned to you
Further and further away you'll see

May God damn me
That I do not mean that

-There is no going back

Never a time can be recalled
EVER in my life
That I said "I love You."
People nowadays
Just LOVE to toss the word around
It ruins everything

Will that word mean anything at all anymore?
After they have been hurt and severely scarred
No matter how many times
Anyone repeats that word
It will not heal the wounds

In this lifetime
If ever "I love you'
Leaves my lips
Anyone to receive them
Will know that I meant it...

Redeem my life!
How can I be
My soul was true before?
Feeling the world wanted
Nothing more but honesty
Does anyone ask for it
At all anymore
My answers to you were
But the truth
No matter how bitter
Or sweet

After finishing the last drop of this bottle I held,
a portal opened through my eyes.
Of whatever I could do? To change the past.
How everything before was wrong turned right.
If only!
But most likely.
Everything would be played like a video game.
Where right is wrong and wrong is right.

-No feeling of consequences

Across the bar
The sight of you drinking
Uncontrollably
The look in your eyes
Had an avalanche of tears
That slid ever so slowly...

Staying in what we call 'the comfort zone'
Exists the meaning for reasons
But how do people cope?
Some spend time with family at home
Others are soothed by loud music
Comfort keeps everyone busy

Now for the discomfort
Some smoke a cigarette
Some lock themselves in
Alone at home
Discomfort stops everyone to be busy

I however see both sides
For I am always
Comfortable being uncomfortable

I promised myself
To change my life and do better
This week and the last
That promise will probably
Be on my to-do-list forever
There's no way of staying on path with me
Somehow everything feels stuck
Like I am pushing on a pull door

Out of every conversation
I've had with a man here sitting at my table
Without any doubt knowing
I am under the influence
One question I tend to sneak during discussion
About these so-called "love of our lives"

why do you love her?
Always with no hesitation answered
"Because she is beautiful!"

A beautiful woman is one thing
What makes her beautiful then?
My thoughts on this subject need answers

In return for my questions
The blankest stare is given back
From a man asked something
So simple...

Many will say sorry
Before feeling
The absolute need to kill yourself
Just to make it all stop!
No human should ever
Conclude to that point in life

That is why we are here tonight!

-Have one on me, friend

For the past two hours
The constant praying
For any soul here in this bar
To sit at this table and talk
About anything
Whether it's about your day
Or how good the beer is
Secretly maybe
You spill unforgivable dark secrets
Despite everything
Nothing seems to work

The closest I felt
To ever loving a woman
Was when I told her
We can not see each other again
After giving reason
I got into my car
And cried every single tear built up over the years
Questioning the entire time

Is missing someone?
The same as ever loving someone?

Feeling cold quite often
It starts from the feet
Then to the hands and fingers
I'd better take another shot of this vodka
Before the cold hits my heart
My back faces you
But I feel your presence fill this bar
Like a winter storm impossible to ignore
Your eyes are stinging in the back of my head
I know it!
But I refuse to look back
Knowing the outcome if we ever made eye contact
I would be a frozen ice block

Hand me the entire bottle
It will warm me up so much more

One day I ever
Asked you to disappear
With me

To build a new life
From the ground up
And live in our log cabin
Comforted by a warm fireplace
Surrounded by a calm snowfall
Under the northern lights

Would you?

Must nowadays
Everybody control the need
To not be selfish
As it were ever a bad thing?

Selfishness can define you
Your authenticity
Your desire of life
To carry yourself

When you have this drink with me
I want you to be selfish
It's ok

"Excuse me, why do you always look down and never forward? Is there something wrong?" she said.

"No, everything is right" saying back

"Well then what is it? You seem sad?"

I am happier staring down at the blank ground
Then looking up to a sad miserable world.

-The world around is sad, NOT you

My wandering thoughts
Slowly began to lead my mind back
Into reality
The matter fact that I
Have been in this bar day after day
More than times ever counted
This bar is my prison of choice

Ever since the contact with me stopped
From the love of my life
Or even my own family
I've considered remaining here

The people here talk to me
And tend to care what happens in my life
The best part is
You can have all you can drink!

Growing discomfort:

Every day that passes
I think about
When will life
Throw me my daily bread
To spark and feed my mind
To give purpose that's true and fulfilling

I've envisioned a table and plate
Sitting in front of me
With other people surrounding
With the same table and plate

Life posing as the server
Handing full loaves to most
And a slice to few
Then passing leaving my plate empty
I take and accept
Being alive is enough
To thank life for

-The starvation will come later

I could take you with me
But my stay here with you
Is momentary
After putting my coat on
She grabbed my hand tight
And very persuasively
She says to me
Then I will take you
And keep

Without a doubt
Knowing the outcome for tomorrow
I could never say no
To her glistening blue eyes

You don't have to say anything

It's nice to just breathe
Together comfortably in silence

With one another's company
While sharing drinks

What kills the moment
Are your eyes glued on your phone

That is the worst silence to sit through

How can someone love at all?

If they cannot possibly love themselves

-put yourself first sometimes

Any given choice to me. Whether I decide to live in the real world or in MY world.
You see the world I live in is where people come at night and sleep during daylight.
MY world is calm and quiet
Everything is peaceful
As it should be
Despite the world, my existence takes place in
I can live and do whatever I want.

-You make the choice, do not let life make the choice for you

THE HATEFUL

If there is one thing in this world
That I can ever trust
It's ME
And only me
Sober or a complete drunken mess
Bottom line is
My mind will always remain true
To me

Same bar
Just a different Friday evening
May another cliché night out commence
Starting with taking the same seat in the corner
Order one pitcher of lager
Then count the heads of the house regulars

Until a companion of the opposite sex
Looks your way
Directly where eyes will lock in
And two adults see each other alone

That is when decisions will be made
Either they play the night out solo
Or partake in the selfish deed for one another
Till the next morning

-either way, my night will be made

If ever I wanted
To play with your feelings
Get exactly what I want from you
And take it all
I absolutely could

Sometimes I see life as a game
A very dangerous game
That I play pretty damn well

Lately the weight on my shoulders
Got heavier
Even though I carry nothing
The thoughts in my head
Create a growing pressure
That feels more painful than I can bear
My issue is
I am only thinking one thing
Constantly!

I don't want anything at all from this world
Reason being
This world wants some things for the wrong reasons,

-quid quo pro

Anybody I think of, really likes movies

But that doesn't mean they should treat life as one

I was always raised to listen to the old and wise.
Nowadays, others that are young listen to the young,
And get nowhere

-dead future

This whole not feeling anything
An emotional numbing sensation
Is really beginning to sting

FAIR WARNING
Tonight ladies
When you all set foot
Through these doors
And consider acknowledging me
Classifying me as a nice guy?
Or a bad guy?
The warning is I am neither
Nor in between

- What am I to you tonight?

Nothing

And I mean NOTHING

In this world
Seems to feel good anymore

Wait till night falls
All my demons will soon arise
From the depths of my heart

Wait till night falls
When these hateful words
Spill from my mouth

Just so you wait tonight darling
YOU asked for the real me?
You will receive it

My approach to you
Will be followed by dark clouds
And violent roars of thunder
I will be

The devil that walks into church

We are all puppets to man
But children to God

Unrelatable Party:

Get up and socialize
Talk to someone about something
Ask them about THEIR day
And about THEIR life
Its ok,
Fake your feelings of interest
To act like you care
When in reality

Who cares anymore?

All of my life
I've been patiently waiting
For love and connection to find
Until one day my patience drained
After scouring the earth
For the love dreamt of
Only to figure after all this time
The love and connection
Dreamt of happening to me
Never existed
And NEVER will.

Intentionally
I would never hurt anyone

But I always leave
A little scar
To just about anyone I meet

Our friendship
Recently seems to have sunk down
Your tight hugs to me now
Feels hollow
Your ears no longer work
When I speak

The minute I order these two drinks
For us
Your heart and soul sing hellfire
We laugh throughout the night
While making plans for the near future

Once the drinks stop rolling in
We split back into our different lives
Forgetting what we said
And what we shared
I do still know your name however
My friend!
You are just an acquaintance to me now

Good company is often hard to come by
Especially for yours truly
All that is given to me
Is a violent stare
One gentleman decided to share with me
All evening to nearly closing
My decision was to share back
With a proper response

"One of two things happens with that glare sir"
"Either you are absolutely falling in love with me"
"Or you want to murder me"

"And I highly fucking doubt that you are in love"

-A drunken man with a vendetta

The Clueless Mind:

You are smart
But somehow you can't see red
The flags this man in your sight has shown
You've completely ignored
De ja vu must be on my side
I wouldn't even take a wild guess
If I didn't know better
When he leaves you for his next victim
Your comfort is to find another him
This endless cycle will end until your older days
By then
But now
It has to stop
Let me help you at least
To ease your pain
After what you've been through
We can help each other
Over these two glasses and a full bottle

Come to find out
It's one hundred percent true
How this world focuses on your flaws
Instead of what was achieved
However so, to you woman
Your flaws
are what I admire about you

If only you knew that

I WANT to help this woman
I wish nothing more but the best for her
My reason being
The man you are with
Has helped himself more to you
Then actually helping YOU
I hope one day
That you would just open your damn eyes
And see through clearly
This person defined to you as a man
Is not a man
But a burden shaped like a human
Now that day has come
After all my energy
Hoping and praying the best for you
Has come to an absolute end
When I saw another burden
Stuck on your side
Walking and holding your hand
Something cold shot into my heart
It's either disappointment
Or my body telling me
To completely forget the thought
To ever help you

-Do people ever change?

In the event my brain signals my heart
Telling me she is not worth it?
And does not deserve my time
I will walk away, plain and simple

-A Gemini man's soul

Popularity and Judgement:

Envious to see
People smiling, laughing amongst themselves
Feasting and drinking with the King
Who is providing the joy that spreads to all who's sided with him

Whatever that made them laugh must be hysterical
Boy, what must I do to get a taste
To site with the King
To truly smile and laugh to his amusements

Until I felt the dozen eyes settle in my direction along with pointing fingers
Hearing the whispered gossip about my empty table and dark clothes
Clarity was sudden, like sharp ice
That I was the King's amusement flaunted to his peasants

She's seen me here
Every Friday night
Then she asked
"Why are you?'

My response
"For some reason being here
Feels like home"

Outside of this establishment
I do not have a home

-Home is where you can be yourself

I do not mind listening
Of what you have to say
Is that not why we are here?

Exchanging life stories over drinks
To actually listen to each other
And not just hear

But so far
Everything you told me
About all of your problems
Sounds like you haven't been hurt enough

The thought of you
Meant something one point
Speaking wonderful things
And sharing memories to everyone
Of us

It really just showed me
How much you were important
And loved

On my day of marriage
However we decide
To live our lives
No matter how much
You show hate or love
Death WILL part us

I met a man one night
A man never seen in this bar before
The pierced look of his eyes
Showed absolutely no fear
No true emotion of heart

This man whispered with his head down low
Stating he believes in God's existence
But puts no faith in him
If there ever was a human on earth
That should be feared
It's a man that has nothing to lose or gain

The thought to put these words together
Made me want to take another drink
After that refreshing taste of whiskey
I looked up
Into the mirror hanging in the bar
The man defined as godless and fearless
Was me looking at my reflection

Anytime I help myself
It never helped the world
It's like destruction passing my every direction
Then again
This world has NEVER helped me
I will continue to help me
And let the world self-destruct

Been here since opening hours
Slowly sipping on cold Devil's Cut
To the point it turned room temp
Then a young woman and her friends offered
To play a game of cards with them
Called 'Never have I ever"
Sounds intriguing!

When the first card was pulled
I could tell this woman's question
Was going to be directed to me
"Never have I ever kissed a woman"
Not one drink from anyone was attempted

Her question and my silent answer
Momentarily paused the game
I now feel the piercing eyes
Turn into sudden judgement
Then again I thought

It's only a game...

I willingly surrender my confession to you
I eat my heart out for you and spill my blood
The moment you entered through those doors
Your presence instantly lit a fire in my soul
Burning violently like Hell's never-ending inferno
Your beauty absolutely blinded me like the sun
That fill the sky with bright light in the summer
Your personality greatly shows true kindness
Genuine like the angels' purpose here on earth
Your voice is comforting like a soothing rainfall
Whenever you speak the spotlight shines on you
People seem to love you no matter what you do
Our one-time conversation turned into several
Asking myself every time and minute that goes by
While I sit with you woman, sipping vodka
How come this gorgeous masterpiece of a princess
Is talking to a disturbed lonely beast as myself
God must have sent her to me
Even though my prayers were absent for years
She was what I defined as God's perfect creation
An Angel in disguise to remove my burdens
And erase the memories of the horrible past

Or so I thought...

Wanting to believe
What you are saying to me now
And wanting to believe
to ever hear from you again
I know
What you are feeling now
You won't be feeling tomorrow
It's better to play this night out with you
Until closing hour
After that
You are now nothing more but a memory

THE HOPE
TO HEAL

Devil's Hour:

Isn't it true?
3 am at night
The soul wanders
Playing show and tell
Of our past
Revealing
The skeletons in our closet
Tonight, my skeletons
Will come alive as zombies

Whatever life will throw your way
To test your capabilities
Man or woman, take it
Try to hide the pain
Learn to live with the splinter
If ever anyone needs to be doctored
I know the name
Of a famous medicine man
His name is Jack Daniels

The distance
Between our bar stools
Seem so far away
But you are in view

And in view
Your head is bowing
Your right hand with a drink
And the other wiping tears off your face

Whatever you're going through
Must be painful and agonizing
It is reflecting to me
Like what you feel, I'll soon feel
Please... stop

Trauma should not be held forever
At what time will it ever fade?
To be forgotten

Every scarring memory starts to fade
The more I abuse this substance
Then I just let it all go away

Meanwhile
The entire world
Holds their scarring memories sober

Alive and well
Or six feet under
I feel you will
See me again
This life or the next
Some way, somehow

You may not think they'll remember now
Just wait until they grow up

-To the alcoholic parents

Smiles can be scary sometimes

She

Wears a smile
and nothing else

You've told me

Depression is slowly consuming you
The look you gave
Was a hint for me
To comfort you
Maybe try to fix
What all I can do?
If what you feel is what I feel

When showing fake emotion

Every time it stings me

When exposing true emotion
It inflicts on others hurtfully

That gives me power!

The only dreams I want to see tonight
Are the ones where I'll remember in the morning
About a life never lived before
Or even where I'm flying in the air at night

How will I get there fast enough?
I am already half a bottle down
And yet to feel anything
To get closer to my dreams...

What does anyone resort to?
When there is nothing left for themselves

-Your friend, Midnight Whiskey...

If ever this place closed down
Forever permanently
My future self will never find another
The walls of this bar
Have heard my stories
My every secret
More than Satan himself
Question is
Will this establishment
Ever find another me?

A part of me
Wants to let loose to feel something great!
Then the other part
Warns me why it's a bad idea

-self-control

If it wasn't for your company tonight
My wandering peaceful thoughts, would then
Turn into dark violent fantasies
Brother, let's drink to good company…

Morning thoughts:

I'm up now
Leaving this bed now will ruin my day
I should call in sick to work
It'll be my fourth this month

I can never fail to God
I can only fail to myself
What I live for is what I make of it
Despite the obstacles soon to face
I am not leaving this bar
I'll do all my repenting here

Just for one night
Let someone else
Play their broken record

I would rather listen to theirs
Just for a little while
Instead of my own

-listen to others sometimes,
And not always yourself

Let us in peace
To enjoy this cold wonderful lager
And not stare into our corner
Like we are withered plants
That have never been watered

There is one thing that no soul on earth can change. And that is the thoughts in my mind. My heart and soul however change constantly when I am around HER.

I tell myself
That I am this
Fearless, Godless monster

But this girl told me
I am a human-sized teddy bear

Before this establishment closes
Kindly I ask sir for the whole bottle
May I drink to forget my horrid past
Drink to forget my past loves
My presence to this life
The constant pain inflicted on others
Or even myself
May I drink to the point
Where my every feeling is numb by this poison
With no telling my destination
In either a hospital,
Waking up in the clouds standing at a golden gate,
Or surrounded by brimstone and painful screams
However soon it may be, I do tell and ask of anyone
I do not need saving
If you see me lying helpless on this street
Just let me be
Do not pick me up like an injured alley cat in need
I asked for this
Let me pay the price!!!

-Self-pity

It's always the next day
After a fun night out
From your favorite spot at the bar
That will definitely not feel so fun
In the morning...

-Morning consequences

The same woman
Throughout my journey here
Left me a message
Saying she wants to go out
With me
To have more conversations
And exchange drinks as usual
In the same spot
By the lonely bar...

The Lonely Bar is a book that consists of several events of a man spending most nights at his favorite spot in the bar. Specifically, as some have named, the lonely section of the bar. Every single poem leads and builds a story of what all can happen just over a few drinks. When the warm sensation comforts the body, that is when people show the love, or even hate, repressed inside their hearts, just to cope with the loneliness.

I wanted to share these thoughts with the running crowd that has been in my shoes before. I would say to them, "If ever anyone picks up the bottle and consumes every drop, it will not change a thing in life. It will only hurt you the next morning."

I dedicate this book to my brothers I served with that counseled me throughout my darkest times. To the ones I used to know that passed, you are all in my prayers. I guess it's best to be gone now for good reasoning than later as I always said.

Rest easy...

Also, I want to thank my grandfather Paul E Beckworth who I never met. Growing up I always knew your name, but later discovered your voice in poetry. The words in your book "From Sunrise to Sunset" made me understand the obstacles you faced in your life. From being a soldier serving your country in WWII, to being a preacher of a church. I know you kept your faith on the right track to help others get closer to God.

I thank you for your service...

About the Author

Jared Reed is a Texas native, born in Cleburne and raised in Granbury. Over the years and through many obstacles, Jared always wanted to pursue, write and express himself in a book. He served in the U.S Army for nearly 4 years and during that time of substance abuse, he traveled most of Europe.

He always had a notebook with him to constantly write about his experiences and thoughts of every bar he visited. Still on the road to recovery from alcoholism, he will continue to create a series, making this his first book ever published.

Follow Jared on Instagram at jared_c_reed_

www.ingramcontent.com/pod-product-compliance
Lightning Source LLC
Chambersburg PA
CBHW060500080526
44584CB00015B/1497